ALL RONDA

I.S.B.N. 84-378-0865-0

Dep. Legal B. 41961-1988

editorial **escudo de oro, s.a.** Palaudarias, 26 - 08004 Barcelona - Spain

Impreso en España - Printed in Spain
F.I.S.A. Palaudarias, 26 - 08004 Barcelona

Magnificent close-up of Ronda's ramparts.

THE ROMANS' ARUNDA

Ronda occupies a surprising, apparently unlikely location at an altitude of 750 m; in the words of Rainer Maria Rilke, the town is "exuberantly perched on the enormous, perilous promontory of rocks." Its natural setting is extremely, characteristically beautiful. "El Tajo" is a gorge that looks as if it had been cut with a pickaxe, like an open wound inflicted on the earth by some furious giant; La Alameda 'Mirador' — vantage point — is on its very brink, and from here the town dominates a broad, fascinatingly original panorama. In the foreground, the fields stretch over a fertile plain, bathed by the sluggish waters of the Guadalevín; and in the background one can glimpse the rough sierras toying with the horizon. In the precise verses by Dionisio Ridruejo,

*A fine view
of Charles
V's Gate.*

The 'Puerta de Almocabar,' in the 13th-century Arab style.

The church of the Holy Ghost.

'Santa María de la Encarnación la Mayor' church.

Remontando el arroyo
que ha hendido a Ronda y luego
se refugia en los montes
con difíciles quiebros
el alma herida de humildad descubre
el castillo encantado de su ensueño.
Se hizo acción el paisaje
y representa el drama de su esfuerzo.
La impresión es relato
y la vista argumento.

Ronda itself and its surroundings would seem to be a poetic god's dream made reality. Everything around it appears original, unlike any other landscape. It is difficult — especially in the light of modern-day utilitarian logic — to understand how and why the town was built on the site where it stands. Nevertheless, Ronda and its framework present themselves to the traveller like a perfectly conceived and executed painting. Its contemplation astonishes, but once one's sensibility has assimilated its appearance, it is impossible to conceive the town on any site other than the one it occupies, or framed by any other landscape. Ronda is like a miracle of plastic art. Rocks and trees, the river and the land, the countryside and the town, constitute the essential notes in the symphony that is Ronda.

This is one of the most ancient towns in Spain. Judging by what Stephanus Byzantinus wrote five centuries before the Christian age, the history of Ronda's site began with the presence of the Greeks. The fact that coins with designs drawn from Greek mythology

have been found in Ronda, the existence of a place called *Charco Lucero,* which in Greek means "land of vines," at the ancients' Acinipo (a Roman municipality 19 km from Ronda at a spot known as Ronda la Vieja), and other traces strengthen the hypothesis that the Hellenes trod these lands before the Romans did.

However that may be, it was Rome that conferred on Ronda its definitive, illustrious historical protagonism. *Arunda* — the Romans' name for Ronda — was very important as a trading centre in *Betica,* Roman Andalusia. Recent archaeological investigations seem to have confirmed the theory that the famous city called *Munda* was situated on the site of present-day Ronda. The town's Roman ancestry is, in any case, corroborated by the numerous monuments that are still retained, perfectly conserved.

It could be said of Ronda — as of Córdoba — that the town is half Roman, half Arab. It was conquered by the Arab leader Zayde Abn Kesadi Al Sabsaki in 711; the Moslems called the town *Runda,* and their domination over it continued until 1485. The occupation left innumerable interesting traces in this regional capital. The ancients' *Arunda* even became capital of a Mohammedan kingdom for a while, in Omar-ben-Hafsun's time.

After being reconquered by King Ferdinand the Catholic on May 22nd 1485, Ronda was where the subject Moslems' last rebellion broke out. Under Christian rule the town continued to play a worthy rôle in history, as is demonstrated by the many buildings of unquestionable architectural value dating from after 1485: the most remarkable are the 'Casa de

Row of balconies and columns; choir-stalls and choir ('Santa María la Mayor' Collegiate Church).

The Town Hall façade; Arab minaret.

Mondragón,' the Marquis of Salvatierra's House, the 'Puente Nuevo' ('New Bridge'), the Church of the Holy Ghost, and the Collegiate Church of Santa María la Mayor (which was previously a mosque).

Ronda also played a significant part in the War of Independence: its inhabitants struggled with exceptional courage against the French troops. The following period was one where intrepid smugglers and audacious bandits became minor protagonists of history, and Ronda was more or less a romantic capital of tearaway figures in the first half of the 19th century.

*Image of
Our Lady of
Peace,
patron saint
of Ronda.*

'Santa Isabel de los Angeles' convent.

'Marquis of Salvatierra's House': façade. ▷

Among the distinguished historians who have dealt with the time-honoured lineage of Ronda we must at least mention Strabo, Titus Livius, Aben-Jaldun, Aby-Abd-Allad, Hernán Pérez del Pulgar, Padre Mariana, Modesto Lafuente and Vicente Espinel.

Numerous novelists and poets, both Spanish and foreign, have also concerned themselves with Ronda, from Prosper Mérimée (who situated some episodes of his popular novel *Carmen* in the town) or Dionisio Ridruejo (author of the extraordinary *Cancionero de Ronda,* who was imprisoned here for some time) to Azorín, Pío Baroja and Blasco Ibáñez. The great poet Rainer Maria Rilke wrote several poems in Ronda, in-cluding *The Spanish Trilogy, The Resurrection of Lazarus* and *Ariel, Spirit of the Air.*

Among the many illustrious natives of Ronda, the most outstanding include Hamed el Zegri, who was governor of the town and defended the plain of Málaga when that city was besieged by King Ferdi-nand the Catholic — he later defended Málaga itself, and demonstrated his bravery against opponents far superior in numbers so often that his name is perpetuated in that of a street in Málaga; and Omar Ibn Hafsun, born at Torrecilla (Parauta), a hamlet in the midst of the sierra — the famous leader who sparked the most important uprising against the

Plaza de la Duquesa de Parcent.

caliphate and maintained his stronghold in the impregnable fortress of Bobastro until his death. Mention should also be made of Abuldeca, an Andalusian Arab poet of the 13th century; of Vicente Espinel, the poet, novelist and musician, to whom the addition of the fifth string of the guitar is attributed; of Antonio de los Ríos Rosas, an outstanding politician who became President of Congress; and of Francisco Giner de los Ríos, a prestigious educator, follower of Krause philosophy and professor of Philosophy of Law, who exerted great influence on public affairs in Spain in the last quarter of the 19th century and the beginning of the 20th, and founded the 'Free Educa-

tion Institute' in 1876. Nor should we forget Cristóbal de Polo, the creator of ''El Polo,'' genuine music of Ronda; or the great stars of bullfighting who were born in Ronda, such as Francisco Romero, his son Juan and his grandsons José, Antonio, Gaspar and the legendary Pedro Romero who killed 5,500 bulls and whose ballads and couplets have survived to this day; José Ulloa ''Tragabuches,'' very famous as a first-class bullfighter and even more so as a bandit in the sierra; ''Niño de la Palma''; or Antonio Ordóñez, a leading figure in bullfighting for many years, greatly admired by Ernest Hemingway. The historic silhouette of this town of noble lineage stands on the

'Casa de Mondragón': façade.

The Arab Baths.

edge of the sierra; Ridruejo wrote of its unmistakable
characteristics:

> *No queda el oro ni el moro,*
> *pero campea en la cal*
> *el renaciente decoro*
> *del portal.*
> *Mudéjares penitentes,*
> *en el laberinto oscuro,*
> *compran aires suficientes*
> *para la sombra del muro.*
> *Y, manteniendo el empaque*
> *de la mansa soledad,*
> *aún con sus torres da «jaque»*

> *la ciudad.*
> *Valles, montañas, poblados*
> *le rinden toda ufanía,*
> *aunque enreja, silenciados,*
> *bastiones que ayer servía.*

Ronda is not, however, just a town sleeping in
history, good only for provoking nostalgic memories
and impressing the aesthetic sensibility by the artistic
quality of its monuments; but a living metropolis,
populated, breathing deeply the stimulating air of its
sierras and still gladly forging its own dynamic,
fascinating destiny — looking bravely towards the
future.

The 'Moorish King's House': façade.

THE TOWN

"El Tajo" — 'the Cleft' — begins to cut violently into the land at a distance of some 2 km from Ronda. As it comes closer to the town, this incision becomes deeper, attaining — at the vantage point of La Alameda — a depth of 320 m; then it divides Ronda into two parts, formerly joined by the 'Old Bridge' and the 'Arab Bridge,' and connected by the 'Puente Nuevo' since 1788, when this 'New Bridge' was completed (under the supervision of José Martín Aldehuela). The fissure is 160 m deep at this point.

Ronda's original appearance, of beautiful irregularity, is the first thing that calls one's attention as soon as one passes the walls. The town, standing on colossal rocks, occupies a kind of gigantic natural amphitheatre formed by the spurs of the sierras, with which the town's appearance is in harmony of style.

The narrow, winding streets of old Ronda are full of charming surprises for the visitor. When one least expects it, one comes upon the noble, escutcheoned façade of an ancient mansion, or traces of the Romans or Arabs.

The old town extends over three small promontories, forming three quarters that are distinguished by their independent locations more than by anything else, for the town's structure is similar in all three.

The bridges mentioned above — the 'Puente Nuevo' is made up of three arches, 70 m long and 100 m high — lead from the old town to the modern area. This latter is still popularly known as 'El Mercadillo,' because it was the site of the Arab souk. This is modern Ronda: its physiognomy is quite different from that of the old town. The streets are less tortuous, and broader, and flanked here and there by ancestral mansions. The Andalusian character is manifest in the attractively whitewashed façades, in the artistic grilles on the windows, and in the profusion of flowers in pots.

'Casa del Rey Moro': the poetical gardens.

An impressive view of
the 'New Bridge' over
the 'Tajo' gorge.

Wrought-iron grille
enclosing the vantage
points of the 'Puente
Nuevo.'

A view of the 'Old Bridge,' built on the base of the 'Arab Bridge.'

Two splendid views of La Alameda.

The town expands at the beautiful area of La Alameda, from whence one may enjoy broad, poetic views to the horizon. There is a statue of Pedro Romero, the great 18th-century bullfighter from Ronda who became an almost mythical figure in the 'Fiesta Nacional,' in La Alameda; and also a small zoo.

Ronda's bull-ring is very near La Alameda: it is one of the oldest in Spain, and the poet Fernando Villalón called it "the bull-ring of *macho* matadors..." Evocatively colourful "Goyesque corridas" are held in the historic bull-ring at Ronda every year, in the first third of September; the first bullfight of this type was held in Ronda on the occasion of Pedro Romero's second centenary (he was born on November 19th 1754).

Plaza de la Ciudad is another very interesting part of the town; the 'Laurel Castle' used to stand here. This square now features an important ensemble of historic monuments, with the church of 'Santa María de la Encarnación la Mayor,' the Law Courts (once the home of the Catholic Monarchs' son), the Town Hall, the Archaeological Museum, and the Convent of the Order of S Clare.

It is a pleasure both for the eyes and for the spirit to stroll through the streets of Ronda, with traces of history in many places. The town's structure — varied, but always retaining its essential unity — is an

The main gate of the Bull-Ring, a fascinating specimen of the baroque style.

A magnificent view of the arena in the Bull-Ring.

unending source of temptation for the stroller. One wonders what there may be at the end of this or that street, at the top or at the bottom of such-and-such a steep, uneven slope. One feels lively curiosity to see how a particular perspective is completed by the town, or the way in which it gives onto the open panorama that one barely glimpses at the end of a road where the horizon is blurred, almost obscured, by buildings that look ready to leap at one another and start a bitter struggle....

The fact that the countryside and the sierra are constantly visible from any angle is by no means the least of Ronda's charms; the town is thus liberated from the prison of stone, cement and bricks that has enclosed other ancient, beautiful cities. Ronda, on the contrary, is a town of open horizons.

Statue of Pedro Romero, the great bullfighter from Ronda.

MONUMENTS IN RONDA

Ronda and its district retain many vestiges bearing witness to the area's illustrious history. There is a considerable wealth of monuments in the town: traces of the Romans, Arabs and Christians are particularly abundant.

The whole of Ronda, however, is really a monument — a town of incomparably original appearance, in perfect harmony with the natural features supporting and surrounding it. One must view, and assimilate the aesthetics of, the town and its framework as a whole if one wishes to comprehend the artistic value of Ronda's beauty. It would be inconceivable to apply a scholastic point of view here, establishing artificial differences between the parts that make up the struc-

An impressive perspective of
the 'New Bridge' and the 'Tajo'
gorge.

Ronda Casino, formerly the Artists' Circle.

ture of the town and environs. One has to try to take in the ensemble and interpret it as an uncompromisingly united whole. All elements are essential in the ensemble of monuments at Ronda.

SANTA MARIA LA MAYOR

This church stands on the same ground-plan as the previous Moslem mosque. Santa María la Mayor displays in its architecture a mixture of the Gothic and Renaissance styles: the nave and nave-aisles, built in the 16th century, are Gothic, while the arms of the transept and the presbytery date from the 17th century and are in the Renaissance style. The slender tower presents three successive sections, each in a

different style: Mudejar, Gothic and Renaissance. The magnificent choir-stalls are also Renaissance in style; the elegant horseshoe arch in the church denotes its Arab origin.

The Catholic Monarchs consecrated Santa María la Mayor to Catholic worship in the same year that Ronda was conquered.

CASA DEL REY MORO

The building popularly known as the 'Moorish King's House' is not in fact the one where Hamed el Zegri resided: he lived in the 'Casa de Mondragón.'

The 'Moorish King's House,' which belongs to the Duchess of Parcent, is a beautiful, lavishly furnished

The façade of 'Nuestra Señora del Socorro' church.

The room in the Hotel Reina Victoria occupied by the poet in 1913, now converted into the Rilke Museum.

Doorway of the old 'Posada de las Animas,' where the author of Don Quixote stayed.

The statue raised in honour of the great poet Rainer Maria Rilke, located in the gardens of the Hotel Reina Victoria.

CASA DE MONDRAGON

'Mondragón House' has a beautiful Renaissance façade; the two interior courtyards and their respective galleries are also of unquestionable interest. A visit to this building causes a strange sensation of being transferred, as it were, to times past, to a world whose culture one can barely perceive intuitively, but which is overwhelmingly human.

This house was inhabited — before it was rebuilt — by the Arab king of Ronda, first, and later by the Catholic Monarchs. The architecture and history of the building are conducive to flights of the imagination.

THE BULL-RING

The bull-ring was built in 1748 by the Royal 'Maestranza' (equestrian society of noblemen) of Ronda, the oldest in Spain, founded by Philip II in 1572 and closely linked to the origins of bullfighting. The ring's pleasant, elegant architecture, combined with its distinguished history, make it one of the most popular and important monuments in Ronda's heritage. Its lineage is apparent in the baroque style of the main doorway, outstandingly graceful, supported by slender columns. There is a handsome balcony of artistic wrought iron above this doorway. The whole bull-ring is a consummate model of agility and harmony, in which space and architecture are combined with unusual felicity.

The most famous, authentic representatives of the Ronda school of bullfighting gave consummate demonstrations of tauromachy here, from Pedro Romero — the most artistic of his dynasty, who drew up the five rules of this prestigious manner of bullfighting — to Antonio Ordóñez, the matador who was a friend of Hemingway and to whom the novelist devoted pages of praise; and Cúchares, Paquiro and other great bullfighters.

residence with a valuable collection of works of art in the interior. There is a very interesting stairway — with 367 steps cut in the bare rock — leading to the very edge of Ronda's deep "Tajo" or gorge. The beautiful gardens (belonging to the 'National Artistic Treasure') on the brink of the stream exude poetic charm.

CASA DEL MARQUES DE SALVATIERRA

The 'Marquis of Salvatierra's House' is a handsome building with a Renaissance façade. The large balcony — in the same style — displays interesting reliefs with Inca designs.

A perspective of Carrera de Vicente Espinel.

Fernando Villalón dedicated a popular poem to Ronda Bull-Ring; these verses are extracted from it:

> *Plaza de piedra de Ronda,*
> *la de los toreros machos:*
> *pide tu balconería*
> *una Carmen cada palco,*
> *un Romero cada toro,*
> *un maestrante a caballo*
> *y dos bandidos que pidan*
> *la llave con sus retacos...*
> *Plaza de toros de Ronda*
> *la de los toreros machos.*

OTHER MONUMENTS

Within the extraordinary wealth of monuments conserved in Ronda, mention should be made — however schematically — of sights as unquestionably interesting as, for example, the ramparts, the church of the 'Espíritu Santo' (Holy Ghost) built by the Catholic Monarchs to commemorate the conquest of Ronda, the 'Roman Bridge,' the 'Arab Bridge,' the 'Posada de las Animas' where Miguel de Cervantes himself stayed, the Arab Baths, the Convent of S Francis, Philip V's Arch, and the 'Sillón del Moro.' Also: Almocabar Gate — a 13th-century Arab work;

Part of Ronda.

S Sebastian minaret (14th-century); 'Christ's Arch'; the 'Gate of Images' — a vestige of Ronda's 13th-14th-century Arab defences; the 'Casa de la Calle del Gigante' — a 14th-century Arab dwelling; and the 'New Bridge.'

RILKE'S ROOM AND MUSEUM

The room occupied by Rainer Maria Rilke in the Hotel Reina Victoria in 1913 has been converted into a museum, with various articles (books, photographs, letters, etc.) relating to this great poet. The room — number 34 — is kept just as it was when Rilke lived here. The poet paid 7.50 pesetas a day for his full board.

In the patio of the hotel there is a full-length statue of the author of *Poems to the Night,* looking towards the hills.

Rilke's Room/Museum is another of the many tourist attractions in Ronda.

HOLY WEEK IN RONDA

The Easter celebrations in Ronda are impregnated with the emotional passion characteristic in all Andalusia, where the population participates directly, as actors and spectators simultaneously, in the festivities of Holy Week. In Ronda, however, the religious fervour that dominates and channels the processions is made all the more authentic by a kind of spiritual restraint.

The *pasos* — floats — are less spectacular than in

Philip V's Arch and the 'Sillón del Moro.'

The popular 'Fountain of Eight Jets.'

other cities, but the brilliance that makes them popular is by no means lacking. The *cofradías* — brotherhoods — in Ronda include those of *Jesus praying in the Garden, Jesus on the Column, Jesus led to His Martyrdom, Most Holy Christ of Blood, Ecce Homo,* and *Christ of the Remedies;* their members devoutly bear these images — some of them carvings of great artistic value — through the streets, and the atmosphere is filled with the aromatic scent of incense. The artistic effect is very colourful: it enters through the eyes and stimulates the spirit, producing results that are difficult to suppress rationally.

The whole of Ronda lives out the solemn religious event during the Holy Week celebrations. The streets are decked out, but the processions take place

without stridence — the popular fervour is tempered by the liturgy. Many strangers, especially foreign tourists, generally come to see this beautiful spectacle.

BULLFIGHTING

Bullfighting enjoys a long, prestigious tradition in Ronda, going back as far as the 16th century. The introduction of the *muleta* or scarlet cloth to the art is attributed to Francisco Romero of Ronda, the father of the legendary Pedro Romero, author of the phrase whereby "Fear gores more than bulls." It was the Ronda school (which is in rivalry with that of Seville to this day) that gave dignity to the art of bullfighting, which Pedro Romero synthesized in these five rules:

*The typical
Calle de la
Ermita.*

Porch of the
'Virgen de
los Dolores.

Calle de San Carlos, a popular street.

"1. The matador's honour lies in his never fleeing nor running before the bulls, provided he has sword and *muleta* in his hands.

2. The bullfighter must never jump over the fence after the bull has entered the ring, for this would be no less than shameful.

3. Keep close to the bull and wait tranquilly for the butt, which blinds the bull and there is no way the defeat can be avoided.

4. The matador should rely on his hands, not his feet, and faced with the bull should kill or die rather than save face or humble himself.

5. Keep the feet still and follow the bull, this is the way for the bull to give in and expose itself to be killed."

These five rules have been — and still are — respected by the genuine exponents of bullfighting in the Ronda school. For this reason, and leaving aside the incomparable setting of this ancient arena, to attend a corrida in Ronda bull-ring is to reach the deepest meaningfulness of bullfighting and to penetrate the essence of the popular art of tauromachy. To see a "true" *faena* (the final third of the combat with the bull) at Ronda constitutes an opportunity to witness the consummation of the dramatic human grandeur that palpitates in the red and golden entrails of bullfighting; grandeur, flecked with blood and bathed in Apollonian light, in which death is ever-present, and which García Lorca captured with tragic precision in *Llanto por Ignacio Sánchez Mejías,* possibly his best, most impressive poem:

Por las gradas sube Ignacio

The Chapel of San Miguel de los Curtidores.

con toda su muerte a cuestas.
Buscaba el amanecer,
y el amanecer no era.
Busca su perfil seguro,
y el sueño lo desorienta.
Buscaba su hermoso cuerpo
y encontró su sangre abierta...

("Ignacio climbs up the tiers with all his death on his shoulders. He was seeking the daybreak, and the daybreak did not exist. He seeks his confident profile, and the dream disorientates him. He was seeking his beautiful body and he encountered his opened blood.")

There is perhaps no other bull-ring in the world as suitable as that at Ronda for propitiating the full dimensions of that human tremor — simultaneously Dionysiac and Apollonian — which tauromachy bears with it. The prestige of this arena is reflected in these verses by Adolfo Lozano devoted to the death of the matador Curro Guillén in May 1820:

Ha muerto Curro Guillén,
teniendo tan alta honra,
que si lo ha matado un toro,
lo fue en la plaza de Ronda.

("Curro Guillén died, having such great honour, that if he was killed by a bull, it was in Ronda bull-ring.")

The 'Virgen de Gracia' is the patron saint of the Royal 'Maestranza,' as also of bullfighters. This Virgin was chosen as patroness by the noblemen of the 'Maestranza' on August 3rd 1573. The image is venerated in the humble sanctuary bearing its name, in La Alameda in the old San Francisco quarter.

Convent of S Francis: doorway (16th-century).

Part of Ronda.

Among those who have knelt in front of the 'Virgen de Gracia' before entering the arena at Ronda are Pedro Romero, Curro Guillén, Pepe-Illo, Costillares, Antonio Ordóñez....

FOLKLORE IN RONDA

It is almost impossible to conceive the inhabitant of Ronda without a guitar. It is a profoundly Andalusian custom (although we would say in passing that it is similar, at least in its meaning, to that practised — until recently — in nearly all the regions of Spain) to *rondar* — court — young girls, singing and playing the guitar; and this is closely linked to the "rondeña," a popular form of song related to the fandango, typical — as its name indicates — of the lands of Ronda.

The "rondeña" is simple in tone, slightly teasing, and expresses minor sentiments:

> *Dicen que tienes un pero,*
> *un pero que no es de Ronda;*
> *corre y busca una manzana*
> *que se iguale a tu persona.*

The "rondeña" is essentially a descriptive song:

> *Ni más alta ni más baja*
> *ninguna como mi Ronda,*
> *porque de todas las rajas*
> *la del "tajo" es la más honda.*

The "copla" often assumes an agreeable, madrigalian tone:

> *El día que tú naciste,*
> *nacieron todas las flores*
> *y en la pila del bautismo*

cantaron los ruiseñores.

The "rondeña" amounts to the expression of a robust, healthy people, firmly attached to their roots. "Aniya la Gitana" — Ana Amaya Molina, born in Ronda on September 27th 1855, who died in 1933 and was a great-aunt of the brilliant Carmen Amaya — was a very popular flamenco "cantaora" and "bailaora" (singer and dancer), of great personality as an artist. Paca Aguilera was another famous "cantaora" from Ronda. In 1890 they both sang at the celebrated 'Café de Chinitas' in Málaga.

In a lecture given at the Art Centre in Granada on February 19th 1922, Federico García Lorca said, "I wish to recall 'Romerillo,' the mad spirit 'Mateo,' 'Antonia la de San Roque,' Aniya la Gitana' of Ronda, Dolores 'la Parrala' and Juan Breva…"

Another first-class "cantaor" from Ronda was Cristóbal de Polo, the creator of the "Polos de Tobalo," a type of song popular all over the Serranía.

A view of 'Los molinos del Tajo.'

Houses perched on the brink of the 'Tajo' or 'Cleft.'

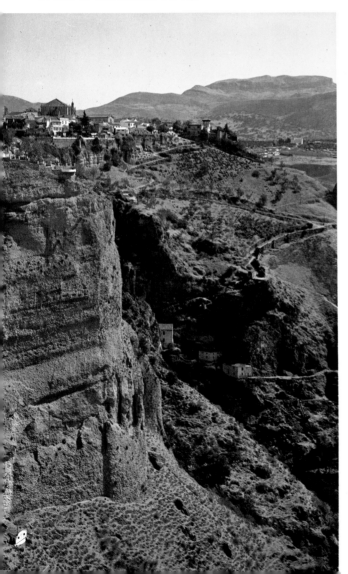

'El Asa de la
Caldera' —
'Cauldron
Handle' —
in the 'Tajo.'

The 'Tajo.'

Part of Ronda, with
its ramparts.

A fine panorama of
Ronda, viewed from
'Don Bosco's
Gardens.'

Two beautiful views of the charming landscape in the valley watered by the river Guadalevín.

CRAFT WORK IN RONDA

Ronda's traditional artisan work is justly famous; it underwent a period of crisis for some years, however, and was on the point of practically disappearing. The work undertaken by the Duchess of Parcent to revive this popular craft tradition was little short of providential: to save it from disappearance, this distinguished lady founded the 'Charitable Institute for Teaching Artistic Skills in Ronda.' But later this organism also ceased to function and Ronda's craftsmen again lacked a centre where they could learn their skills, familiarizing themselves with the techniques of drawing, design and decoration.

Panorama of the
Guadalevín valley.

Puerto del Viento.

Nevertheless, there are still skilful wood carvers in Ronda, whose workshops produce furniture in historical styles, especially in the Spanish Renaissance style. The period furniture made in Ronda displays unmistakably sober, distinguished design. The angles and lines are enriched by good taste, the decorative elements always varied — there is never the slightest hint of shoddy work.

A number of saddlery and harness-making workshops (very few, unfortunately) still survive in Ronda, producing magnificent handmade pieces with fine embroidery and arabesque designs — highly personal and fascinatingly decorative.

From a decorative point of view, the horses' trappings — harnesses, halters, headstalls — and other handmade objects typical of the dwellings in the sierra are also very interesting.

The pottery made in Ronda features a style of its own too, impregnated with delightful primitivism.

GASTRONOMY

Ronda is a town where one can eat superbly. The surrounding area — and the sea of Málaga's Costa del Sol, not far away — produce excellent materials; and the town's location, swept by the winds of the sierra, favours the appetite.

Ronda's cuisine is a serious, honest affair. There are no tricks in the seasoning, no way of fiddling the ingredients. This is a style of cooking suitable for people accustomed to eating as is proper, with dishes prepared specially for robust, restless persons with ample stomachs.

The most outstanding specialities of Ronda's cuisine are roast lamb in the style of the sierra, *chorizos* (salami) *al alcohol,* mutton stew in the Avila style, beef stew with potatoes, fried breadcrumbs with bacon, soups with tomato and garlic, and — naturally — Andalusian gazpacho.

A couple wearing the costume of the sierra; Andalusian dresses with train; and two couples wearing the typical costume of Ronda.

Game merits a section apart. The sierras shelter a great variety of species that, cooked in the Ronda style, would have delighted Rabelais; nor would Brillat-Savarin's refined palate have scorned them. A partridge "al tajo" (cooked with garlic and a special sauce) would reconcile the greatest pessimist with the pleasures of life, especially if it is suitably accompanied with a red wine from Ronda.

There are many bars all over the town where the popular local grape juice is served, on its own or accompanying a dish of *chanquetes,* fresh anchovies, olives or tripe in the Andalusian style, as a *tapa* (hors d'oeuvre); and abundant restaurants where one can restore the energy expended on wandering about the town's steep, irregular streets — with a good meal.

An old kitchen in Ronda; and a large carved chest.

SERRANIA DE RONDA

At a height of 75 m above a level area, the town stands in the centre of an extensive district of *serranía* — hills — of unmistakable appearance. The whole of the area is an intricate complex of passes and villages. The passes (Puerto del Viento, Puerto de Montejaque, Puerto Llano, Puerto de Encina Borracha....) lead to high spots from whence one can always enjoy a broad, rugged panorama; or enable one to descend towards the beautiful, hidden valleys, which seem near to the eyes — displaying their verdure and white villages — but are in fact far away. If one lets one's imagination fly in the realms of more or less fantastic evocation, it is easy to conjure up romantic figures like José María "el Tempranillo" prowling around the sierras on horseback; or the sombre image of José Navarro who, according to Prosper Mérimée, was seduced and so driven mad by "Carmen" that he exchanged his sergeant's stripes for the horse and blunderbuss of a 19th-century bandit.

A series of small villages with Roman or Arab names (Benaoján, Gaucín, Arriate, Montejaque, Jimera de Líbar, Cortes de la Frontera, Alpandeire, Benadalid....) are scattered over the *Serranía*, giving an occasional human touch to its wild landscape.

Despite the primitive physiognomy, full of charm, that these lands conserve, they were settled by man at an early date, as is demonstrated by the cave paintings in Cueva de la Pileta, in the midst of the Sierra de Líbar at some twenty-five kilometres from Ronda. The Romans left traces of their presence in the area: a road, now difficult to make out, along which Pompey and his troops apparently fled towards Carteya (in the province of Cádiz). History and legend mingle in these sierras, forming an aura of myth around Ronda.

Panorama of the Cañada (Ravine) del Cuerno, in the forest of Spanish firs hundreds of years old.

The Spanish firs — conifers that only occur naturally in the Urals and in the Serranía of Ronda — rise towards the sky in the wilds of the sierra.

'Cueva de la Pileta': a magnificent close-up of the lake and three views of the extraordinary cave paintings. ▷

CUEVA DE LA PILETA

The entrance to the 'Cave of the Bowl' is situated at a height of 700 m above sea-level; the walls inside display coloured cave paintings of extraordinary quality, with figures of different animals — in particular bisons, bulls, horses and fishes. The Cave may be reached by taking the road or railway to Benaoján, 23 km from Ronda; from this village there is a road leading to the 'Cueva de la Pileta,' some 4 km away.

Awareness of the cave's existence, and its study, were initiated in 1911 by Colonel Willoghaby Vernet, a British ornithologist who was travelling in the *Serranía* of Ronda in search of the eggs of birds of prey. In the villages of the *Serranía* he was told that there was a place known as the 'Bats' Cave,' discovered some years earlier, located between Benaoján and Jimera de Líbar. Shortly after visiting it, Colonel Willoghaby Vernet published a study of the 'Cueva de la Pileta' in an English journal. When the ar-

'Cueva del Gato,' not far from Benaoján.

Fragments of decorated pottery; spatulas, a burin of bone, a small idol, fragment of a stone bracelet and necklace beads; and different types of stone axes.

chaeologists Obermaier, H. Breuil and Cabré learned of the existence and interest of La Pileta, they decided to visit the cave in 1912, in the company of Colonel Vernet. Three years later they published a well-documented study of the 'Cueva de la Pileta' in Paris, with the support of the Prince of Monaco Foundation and the Paris Institute of Human Palaeontology. The cave began to play an important part in spelaeology and archaeology from then onwards. Its superb cave

Roman statues kept at Ronda Town Hall (Ayuntamiento).

paintings were studied by specialists; and the 'Cueva de la Pileta' was classified as a National Monument on April 25th 1924, the year in which further interesting galleries were discovered. Very important anthropological remains appeared, and in 1926 Pérez de Barradas and Maura, two professors who had studied the newly-discovered galleries at length, published their finds in several journals.

The 'Cueva de la Pileta' is located in a large massif of sedimentary rock similar to that characteristic of the Jura in France. The entrance is in the spacious cave known as the 'Hall of Bats,' where the first wall motifs are: they are pectinate in shape, i.e. like a comb. The majestic central gallery is next, adorned with paintings in red, in authentic Aurignac style. These magnificent paintings are surrounded by grandiose reddish stalagmites: fascinatingly, originally beautiful. The ceiling is over 15 m high — the cave is like a monumental church. The interior is embellished by splendid stalactites and stalagmites, suspended in the air like the tassels of some mythological figure's fantastic tunic. This part of La Pileta causes an indelible impression; one does not know which to admire most, the grandeur of its structure or the quite incomparable beauty characterising it. One's spirit is filled with wonder by this marvel of Nature, located in the bowels of the earth of Ronda province.

After the central gallery there are several more caves, via which one can reach a section known as the ''Salón'' (''Hall''), where the walls are covered with striking, beautiful paintings. This is nothing short of a prehistoric art gallery; within the ensemble of motifs, of admirable quality, the most outstanding are the head of a deer, a horse painted in red, a running elk and a group — painted in red and black — made up of a cow, a goat and several rupestrian-type signs. This Art Hall is situated 200 m from the entrance to the Cave, and at a height of some 713 m above sea-level. The whole gallery displays figures and symbols of original artistic design. This part of La Pileta is one of the most important known centres of prehistoric art. The galleries known as ''Thermopylae'' and the ''Lake Hall'' come after the ''Salón'': they are also of great interest within the ensemble of the 'Cueva de la Pileta.' To complete the fantastic, prehistoric world offered to the visitor's eyes, there is a lake of deep, gloomy water, haunted by an impenetrable mystery of ecology. The lake lies in a deep, black abyss. This would be an ideal setting for a science-fiction film; and yet it is a perfectly real phenomenon, a natural

Roman amphitheatre at the ruins of Acinipo.

Arab pottery articles.

spectacle on which one gazes with fear and wonder. ''The Sanctuary'' is another part that is very interesting in artistic terms. In this gallery one can admire masterly prehistoric paintings depicting different subjects: the most remarkable are a goat drawn with elegant precision, a pregnant mare displaying various signs in red on its body, a cow and a horse sketched with agile carved marks, and several human figures outlined in black strokes. These works constitute a real art treasure, and also precise documentation on the canons of prehistoric plastic arts.

There is a succession of many more caves adorned with paintings, stalagmites and stalactites. The marvellous standard of man-made art and infinite natural beauty impregnating the ensemble of La Pileta does not decline at any stage after entering the Cave. Places of interest that must be mentioned include the ''Hall of the Fish'' (the largest cave in La Pileta, 30 m long, 14 m wide and 12 m high, displaying a striking ceiling, ferruginous in structure, and fine paintings on the flat wall, depicting a fish 1 ½ m long, a little black goat and diverse symbols), the ''Castle,'' the ''Bully's Chamber,'' the ''Moorish Queen's Hall,'' ''The Organs,'' the ''Hall of the Snake,'' the ''Dead Woman'' (where the fossilised skeleton of a woman is conserved), the ''Fairies' Bath''…. These galleries, which are beautifully and variedly decorated, lead to the ''Gran Sima,'' an abyss 62 m deep with a crystalline stalagmite known as the ''Christmas Tree'' in the clay at the bottom.

Arrow-head, phallus, brooches and other bronze articles; and a fragment of a decorated vase in terra sigillata.

TRACES OF ROME

There are Roman remains of great archaeological and historical interest 12 km north of Ronda; the most outstanding parts of the ensemble are "Pompey's Cave" (near which the important Battle of Munda was apparently fought), the circus and the amphitheatre.

In the course of archaeological excavations carried out at the Roman ruins of ancient Acinipo, located at the place known as Ronda la Vieja, many objects were found, in particular a valuable collection of coins (fourteen different specimens have been conserved), pottery pieces, stone tablets and Roman pedestals with inscriptions. The tablets with Roman inscriptions conserved at Ronda are very important; the majority of them were found in the excavations carried out under Rodrigo Aranda's supervision in 1824.

Ronda's history merited the attention of such illustrious Roman personages as Lucius Anneus Florus and Titus Livius (and, earlier, of the famous Greek geographer Strabo); and of Arab historians such as Aben-Jaldun and Aby-Abd-Allad (a Moor from Ronda). Christian historians who dealt with the subject include Hernán Pérez del Pulgar, Jerónimo Franco, Fernando Reinoso Malo, Antonio Campos (author of an index of monuments and curiosities in Ronda and the *Serranía,* which has since been lost), and Juan Rivera Valenzuela. Among modern authors, special mention is due to Federico Lozano and Manuel Oliver, who published the work entitled *Mundo pompeyano,* which won a prize from the Royal Academy of History in 1860.

At the ruins of Acipino there is a very interesting place called "Charco Lucero," where legend has it that

Various coins minted at Acinipo, Malaka and Carteya: Roman quinarii and denarii; different Arab coins; and sestertii dating from the Roman Empire.

winged horses and other monsters emerged from its shores.

Another fascinating spot, similarly shrouded in legend, is 'Cueva del Gato' ('Cave of the Cat'): it is associated with the Roman general Crassus, who formed part of the first triumvirate. It seems that Marcus Crassus was banished as a result of the confrontation between the triumvirs Marius and Sulla. He fled from Rome, eluding persecution by his enemies; and took refuge in Spain, where he was assisted by a landowner of the sierra, Vivio Paciego, who hid him in the 'Cueva del Gato.' The legend has it that Crassus behaved unworthily towards his protector, for when

Roman amphitheatre at Acinipo, in the area known as Ronda la Vieja.

his enemies ceased to pursue him he succeeded in raising an army which not only devastated the whole district of Ronda in their advance towards Málaga, but also laid waste, and robbed, Paciego's properties. Another spot featuring considerable archaeological and historical interest in the Ronda district is the one known as Llanos de Aguayo, north of Los Aguilares, where there was a settlement of which remains still survive; at one stage it had its own temple and necropolis. This is where the Christian troops led by the Marquis of Cádiz camped on May 11th 1485, when Ferdinand the Catholic's army was undertaking the conquest of Ronda.

In contrast with the evocative potency of the mere contemplation of the Roman ruins scattered over the lands of Ronda, the valley dominated by the town, and watered by the Guadalevín, is criss-crossed by beautiful, fertile gardens: the bucolic perspective is further accentuated by the ruggedness of the sierras surrounding the valley. Viewed from Ronda, it seems more like an idyllic corner from some dream rather than a real, tangible piece of land. If one looks further, to the horizon, it seems that the subtle imprecision of the plain might disappear at any moment, engulfed by the threatening avidity of the greyish sierra.

Contents

That ancient part of history which is Spain is often referred to as "the bull's skin", because that is the shape of Spain on the map. The aim of this book is to present a detailed and comprehensive picture of a fragment of that "bull's skin", and to help this it includes a number of spectacular photographs. The Editor will be well satisfied if he has succeeded in giving you a deeper and better knowledge of Spain.

Collection ALL EUROPE

	Spanish	French	English	German	Italian	Catalan	Dutch	Swedish	Portuguese	Japanese	Finnish
1 ANDORRA	•	•	•	•	•	•					
2 LISBON	•	•	•	•	•				•		
3 LONDON	•	•	•	•	•					•	
4 BRUGES	•	•	•	•	•		•				
5 PARIS	•	•	•	•	•						
6 MONACO	•	•	•	•	•						
7 VIENNA	•	•	•	•	•		•		•		
8 NICE	•	•	•	•	•						
9 CANNES	•	•	•	•							
10 ROUSSILLON	•	•	•	•	•		•				
11 VERDUN	•	•	•	•	•						
12 THE TOWER OF LONDON	•	•	•	•							
13 ANTWERP	•	•	•	•	•		•				
14 WESTMINSTER ABBEY	•	•	•	•	•						
15 THE SPANISH RIDING SCHOOL IN VIENNA	•	•	•	•	•						
16 FATIMA	•	•	•	•	•				•		
17 WINDSOR CASTLE	•	•	•	•	•					•	
18 THE OPAL COAST		•	•								
19 COTE D'AZUR	•	•	•	•	•						
20 AUSTRIA		•	•	•	•						
21 LOURDES	•	•	•	•	•						
22 BRUSSELS	•	•	•	•	•		•				
23 SCHÖNBRUNN PALACE	•	•	•	•	•		•				
24 ROUTE OF PORT WINE	•	•	•	•	•				•		
25 CYPRUS		•	•	•	•			•			
26 HOFBURG PALACE	•	•	•	•	•						
27 ALSACE	•	•	•	•	•		•				
28 RHODES		•	•	•							
29 BERLIN	•	•	•	•	•						
30 CORFU		•	•	•							
31 MALTA		•	•	•							
32 PERPIGNAN		•									
33 STRASBOURG	•	•	•	•	•						
34 MADEIRA	•	•	•	•	•						
35 CERDAGNE - CAPCIR		•				•					

Collection ART IN SPAIN

	Spanish	French	English	German	Italian	Catalan	Dutch	Swedish	Portuguese	Japanese	Finnish
1 PALAU DE LA MUSICA CATALANA (Catalan Palace of Music)	•	•	•	•		•					
2 GAUDI	•	•	•	•	•					•	
3 PRADO MUSEUM I (Spanish Painting)	•	•	•	•	•					•	
4 PRADO MUSEUM II (Foreign Painting)	•	•	•	•							
5 MONASTERY OF GUADALUPE	•	•	•	•							
6 THE CASTLE OF XAVIER	•	•	•	•						•	
7 THE FINE ARTS MUSEUM OF SEVILLE	•	•	•	•							
8 SPANISH CASTLES	•	•	•	•							
9 THE CATHEDRALS OF SPAIN	•	•	•	•							
10 THE CATHEDRAL OF GERONA	•	•	•	•							
11 GRAN TEATRE DEL LICEU DE BARCELONA (The Great Opera House)	•	•	•	•	•	•					
12 THE ROMANESQUE STYLE IN CATALONIA	•	•	•	•							
13 LA RIOJA: ART TREASURES AND WINE-GROWING RESOURCES	•	•	•								
14 PICASSO	•	•	•	•	•						
15 REALES ALCAZARES (ROYAL PALACE OF SEVILLE)	•	•	•	•	•						
16 MADRID'S ROYAL PALACE	•	•	•	•	•						
17 ROYAL MONASTERY OF EL ESCORIAL	•	•	•	•							
18 THE WINES OF CATALONIA	•										
19 THE ALHAMBRA AND THE GENERALIFE	•	•	•	•	•						
20 GRANADA AND THE ALHAMBRA (ARAB AND MAURESQUE MONUMENTS OF CORDOVA, SEVILLE AND GRANADA)	•										
21 ROYAL ESTATE OF ARANJUEZ	•	•	•	•	•						
22 ROYAL ESTATE OF EL PARDO	•	•	•	•	•						
23 ROYAL HOUSES	•	•	•	•							
24 ROYAL PALACE OF SAN ILDEFONSO	•	•	•	•	•						
25 HOLY CROSS OF THE VALLE DE LOS CAIDOS	•	•	•	•	•						
26 OUR LADY OF THE PILLAR OF SARAGOSSA	•	•	•	•							

Collection ALL SPAIN

	Spanish	French	English	German	Italian	Catalan	Dutch	Swedish	Portuguese	Japanese	Finnish
1 ALL MADRID	•	•	•	•	•					•	
2 ALL BARCELONA	•	•	•	•	•	•					
3 ALL SEVILLE	•	•	•	•	•					•	
4 ALL MAJORCA	•	•	•	•	•		•				
5 ALL THE COSTA BRAVA	•	•	•	•	•						
6 ALL MALAGA and the Costa del Sol	•	•	•	•	•		•				
7 ALL THE CANARY ISLANDS, Gran Canaria, Lanzarote and Fuerteventura	•	•	•	•	•		•	•			
8 ALL CORDOBA	•	•	•	•	•					•	
9 ALL GRANADA	•	•	•	•	•						
10 ALL VALENCIA	•	•	•	•							
11 ALL TOLEDO	•	•	•	•						•	
12 ALL SANTIAGO	•	•	•	•							
13 ALL IBIZA and Formentera	•	•	•	•							
14 ALL CADIZ and the Costa de la Luz	•	•	•	•							
15 ALL MONTSERRAT	•	•	•	•							
16 ALL SANTANDER and Cantabria	•	•	•	•							
17 ALL THE CANARY ISLANDS II, Tenerife, La Palma, Gomera, Hierro	•	•	•	•	•		•	•			•
18 ALL ZAMORA	•	•	•	•							
19 ALL PALENCIA	•	•	•	•							
20 ALL BURGOS, Covarrubias and Santo Domingo de Silos	•	•	•	•	•						
21 ALL ALICANTE and the Costa Blanca	•	•	•	•	•		•				
22 ALL NAVARRA	•	•	•	•							
23 ALL LERIDA, Province and Pyrenees	•	•	•	•	•						
24 ALL SEGOVIA and Province	•	•	•	•							
25 ALL SARAGOSSA and Province	•	•	•	•	•						
26 ALL SALAMANCA and Province	•	•	•	•				•			
27 ALL AVILA and Province	•	•	•	•							
28 ALL MINORCA	•	•	•	•							
29 ALL SAN SEBASTIAN and Guipúzcoa	•										
30 ALL ASTURIAS	•	•	•	•							
31 ALL LA CORUNNA and the Rías Altas	•	•	•	•							
32 ALL TARRAGONA and Province	•	•	•	•							
33 ALL MURCIA and Province	•	•	•	•							
34 ALL VALLADOLID and Province	•	•	•	•							
35 ALL GIRONA and Province	•	•	•	•							
36 ALL HUESCA and Province	•	•									
37 ALL JAEN and Province	•	•	•	•							
38 ALL ALMERIA and Province	•	•	•	•							
39 ALL CASTELLON and the Costa del Azahar	•	•	•	•							
40 ALL CUENCA and Province	•	•	•	•							
41 ALL LEON and Province	•	•	•	•							
42 ALL PONTEVEDRA, VIGO and the Rías Bajas	•	•	•	•							
43 ALL RONDA	•	•	•	•	•						
44 ALL SORIA	•	•	•								
45 ALL HUELVA	•	•	•								
46 ALL EXTREMADURA	•	•	•	•							
47 ALL GALICIA	•	•	•	•							
48 ALL ANDALUSIA	•	•	•	•							
49 ALL CATALONIA	•	•	•	•							
50 ALL LA RIOJA	•	•	•	•							

Collection ALL AMERICA

	Spanish	French	English	German	Italian	Catalan	Dutch	Swedish	Portuguese	Japanese	Finnish
1 PUERTO RICO	•		•								
2 SANTO DOMINGO	•										
3 QUEBEC			•	•							
4 COSTA RICA	•										

Collection ALL AFRICA

	Spanish	French	English	German	Italian	Catalan	Dutch	Swedish	Portuguese	Japanese	Finnish
1 MOROCCO	•	•	•	•	•						
2 THE SOUTH OF MOROCCO	•	•	•	•	•						

SEVILLA

GRANADA

CADIZ

ALAMEDA

CUEVAS DE SAN MARCO

FUENTE DE LA PIEDRA

SIERRA DE YEGUAS

EL TORCAL

ARCHIDONA

CAMPILLOS

PEÑARRUBIA

ANTEQUERA

CAÑATE LA REAL

VILLANUEVA DE LA CONCEPCION

PERIANA

CUEVAS DEL BECERRO

CASABERMELA

COLMENAR

ARDALES

ALMOGIA

CARRATRACA

ALORA

VELEZ-MALAGA

RONDA

PIZARRA

TORROX

CASARABONELA

CARTAMA

NERJA

ALHAURIN EL GRANDE

MALAGA

TORRE DEL MAR

BENAJARFE

RIO GUADIARO

GAUCIN

MIJAS

TORREMOLINOS

RINCON DE LA VICTORIA

BENALMADENA

CASARES

MARBELLA

FUENGIROLA

ESTEPONA

SAN PEDRO DE ALCANTARA

The printing of this book was completed in the workshops of FISA - Industrias Gráficas, Palaudarias, 26 - Barcelona (Spain)